THE
BOOK
OF
Santa Claus

To: Sue

From: Santa
2007

THE BOOK OF Santa Claus

Vicky Howard

**Andrews McMeel
Publishing**

Kansas City

This edition published in 2004 by the Special Markets Division
of Andrews McMeel Publishing.

The Book of Santa Claus copyright © 2002 by Vicky Howard.
All rights reserved. Printed in Hong Kong. No part of this book may be
used or reproduced in any manner whatsoever without written
permission except in the case of reprints in the context of reviews.
For information, write Andrews McMeel Publishing, an Andrews McMeel
Universal company, 4520 Main Street, Kansas City, Missouri 64111.

ISBN: 0-7407-5134-4

www.vickyhoward.com

Preface

As an artist, I have long admired the beautiful
illustrations that adorn Victorian postcards. An album
of cards collected by my husband's grandmother Nellie first
inspired my passion for collecting. A teacher in the early 1900s,
Nellie received lovely postcards on many occasions from her
students. But it was the Santa Claus cards that stood out from
the others, radiating Christmas joy and capturing my heart.
Over the years I have collected thousands of cards printed during
what is called the "Golden Age of Postcards," from 1898 to 1918.
The Santa Claus images highlight my collection and showcase
the work of the most talented artists of the period. A majority
of the early cards are unsigned, so many wonderful artists
remain anonymous. The most collectible cards are by artists
whose works are signed, such as Frances Brundage and
Ellen Clapsaddle. They were among the first women to
forge careers as commercial artists in the late 1800s,
and their beautiful illustrations of Santa recall
a nostalgic time and live on to be
enjoyed by all of us. ✧

INTRODUCTION

$\mathcal{Y}$es, there is a Santa Claus. And as a newspaper editor reassured eight-year-old Virginia O'Hanlon in 1897, "He exists as certainly as love and generosity and devotion exist, and you know they abound and give to your life its highest beauty and joy."

We can never outgrow the anticipation of a visit from Santa Claus. He is a magical figure, drawn from the legends, history, and folklore of many countries. Over the centuries he evolved from a stern saint to the jolly character we know and love today. The legend of Santa Claus in America had its beginnings in 1822 when Clement C. Moore wrote his poem "A Visit from St. Nicholas" as a gift to his children. In this enduring classic, which begins with the familiar line "Twas the night before Christmas," Santa is described as a round and jolly figure with twinkling eyes and a "nose like a cherry." His account of Saint Nick's visit in a miniature sleigh pulled by tiny reindeer would inspire artists for decades.

Thomas Nast, a political cartoonist, further developed the figure of Santa Claus in a series of illustrations he created for *Harper's Weekly* over a span of twenty-three years, beginning in 1863. He based his pen-and-ink illustrations on his childhood memories of "A Visit from St. Nicholas." His "Merry Old Santa Claus," below, is one of the most beloved images of Santa ever created. Victorians embraced the jovial character and Santa Claus became a favorite subject for Christmas postcards printed from 1898 to 1918. These cards continue to be the most collected today.

In this book I share my favorite images and poetry from my collection of antique Christmas postcards and books. The beautiful portrayals of Santa capture the magic and true spirit of giving that is the heart of Christmas. ✧

"Merry Old Santa Claus"
By Thomas Nast
Harper's Weekly
January 1, 1881

Who is Santa Claus?

SANTA CLAUS is anyone who loves another and seeks to make them happy; who gives himself by thought or word or deed in every gift that he bestows; who shares his joys with those who are sad; whose hand is never closed against the needy; whose arm is ever outstretched to aid the weak; whose sympathy is quick and genuine in time of trouble; who recognizes a comrade and brother in every man he meets upon life's common road; who lives his life throughout the entire year in the Christmas spirit.

– Edwin Osgood Grover, 1912

Illustration by Frances Brundage, 1

I still believe in Santa Claus!
Though years and years have flown,
Whene'er the Christmastide comes round
I find I have not grown.

You tell me now that I'm a man,
'Tis time for wiser things;
I grant it all, and yet, child-like,
I wait for what love brings.

Do you believe in Santa Claus?
Of course, of course you do!
Faith, hope and love, they still abide
In that big heart of you.

– Henry Victor Morgan, 1922

Printed in Germany, 1912

We can't forget old Santa Claus,
His kind and jolly face;
In Christmas love and giving, too,
He holds an honored place.

He's Santa Claus to everyone,
Young, aged, rich and poor;
No Christmas day could be complete
Without him I am sure.

– Maye Currier Minard, 1926

Printed in Germany, 1915

I ask my little girl of three,
"Who's Santa Claus, I'd like to know?"
She comes and climbs upon my knee,
And tells me how upon the snow
Old Santa comes, with sleigh and deer,
And though he's big and chimney small,
He manages to get in here
And fill the stockings, one and all.

I asked a Grandpa white with snow,
"Who's Santa Claus, if such there be?
You've surely had a chance to know,
And when he came what did you see?"
"There's Santa Claus in every heart
That is at peace with all mankind,
That love bestows and gifts impart—
Old Santa is not hard to find."

– Alson Secor, 1912

nted in Germany, 1910

Design Copyright 1910 by Frances Brundage

Christmas Greetings.

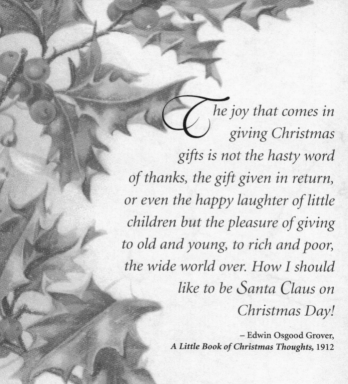

The joy that comes in giving Christmas gifts is not the hasty word of thanks, the gift given in return, or even the happy laughter of little children but the pleasure of giving to old and young, to rich and poor, the wide world over. How I should like to be Santa Claus on Christmas Day!

– Edwin Osgood Grover,
A Little Book of Christmas Thoughts, 1912

Don't leave it all to Santa
As the Christmas days draw near,
But look about for a chance
To multiply Yule-tide cheer;
Santa needs your assistance
The Christmas needs to relieve,
And remember it is always
More blessed to give than receive.

– *Choice Christmas Entertainments*, 1924

A HAPPY CHRISTMAS

WITH BEST WISHES FOR A MERRY XMAS From

Printed in Germany, 1913

SANTA CLAUS

STORY BOOK

When the first frosty snowflakes
begin to float down,

And the wind whistles sharp, and
the branches are brown,

I'll not mind the cold, though my
fingers it numbs;

For it brings the time nearer when
santa claus comes.

– Elizabeth Sile,
Santa Claus Visit, 1890

When Santa sees a hanging
stocking on *Christmas Eve*
he knows he has found someone
who still has faith in him and
who knows what the real
Christmas spirit means.
It is said that a warm welcome
doubles the value of a gift, and
for *Santa Claus*, the sight of an
empty stocking on Christmas Eve
doubles his joy.

– Edwin Osgood Grover, 1912

A merry Christmas

When Santa Claus bestows his gifts on children high and low, May you each year your stocking find well filled from head to toe.

– Christmas postcard, 1909

Printed in Germany, 1914

Stockings do not make a Christmas,

Though they are filled from toe to top

With presents that delight the heart,

From Santa Claus's Christmas shop;

No, though the toys be fine and rare,

Love and kindness must be there,

To make a Merry Christmas.

— Marie Irish, 1931

Here's a merry Christmas may a merry heart Accompany its hours

I hear one ask:
"What pleasure can
Christmas hold for children
who cannot see their gifts or
the sparkling tree or the smile of
Santa Claus?" I answer that the
only real blind person at
Christmastime is he who
has not Christmas
in his heart.

– Helen Keller, 1906

Christmas is not a time or a season but a state of mind. To cherish peace and good will, to be plenteous in mercy, is to have the real spirit of Christmas.

– Calvin Coolidge

The Spirit
of Santa Claus

It's always good for us to pause
And think awhile of Santa Claus—
That jolly symbol we revere
When we approach the changing year.

Behind his beard so long and white,
In which our children take delight,
There beats a heart from color free
Which bids all children "come to me."

– Marshall M. Morgan

Printed in Germany, 1910

Let us give Santa welcome,
Bid him draw near,
Enwreathed with pine and holly,
He brings presents and good cheer!

– *Recitations for Boys & Girls*, 1904

Printed in Germany, 1912

December's here.
From far and near
We hear the sleigh bells jingle
The ground is white,
A splendid sight,
The stars above us twinkle.

We'll offer gifts,
And get them, if
We're good as Santa wishes.
The reindeer swift
Will bring those gifts,
Sleds, dolls, toys, books and dishes.

– *Santa Claus Christmas Book*, 1926

Illustrations by Frances Brundage, 1912

December 31, 1905

My dear little friend:

I have just finished reading your letter. I am glad that you
remembered to write me this year. I don't know whether
I will have enough of the toys and dollies to go around
for which so many of my little friends are asking, but I'll
try to bring you what you asked for in your letter, and
maybe more than that. I am on my way.

Good-bye for now,

Santa Claus

– Mailed from Toyland at Emery, Bird, and Thayer's,
Santa's Kansas City Headquarters, 1905

Illustrations by Frances Brundage, 1915

A JOLLY CHRISTMAS.

Printed in Germany, 1912

Far to the North,
Where not a plant can grow,
Kriss Kringle built his beautiful house,
A palace of ice and snow.

There all the year he works away
For good little girls and boys,
And when Merry Christmas
comes again,
They all can have new toys.

– M. D. Sterling, 1902

Though clouds grow dark and north winds blow,
Though blizzards rage with stormy gale.
Though snow banks pile up high and steep,
Dear Santa's visit never fails.

What matter if the night be dark,
Or if the mercury goes down?
His prancing reindeer are on time
And Santa's sure to be in town.

– Marie Irish

MAY ALL
YOUR
SWEETEST
HOPES COME
TRUE,

Christmas time has come again

And Santa Claus is near,

With reindeer team-a prancing

And sleigh bells ringing clear.

Oh, hear our happy voices sing

To welcome one so dear,

This happy Christmas evening.

– The Merry Christmas Book, 1936

Illustrations by Ellen H. Clapsaddle, 1911
Printed in Germany

Here's to a happy holiday,

*Health and wealth for all the
year round!*

*Saint Nick will be back with
reindeer and sleigh;*

*Let us sing and ring bells till
the echoes resound.*

*We wish you a stocking with
presents stuffed high,*

*And plenty of plums in your
Christmas pie!*

– The Ladies' Home Journal, 1906

Happy, happy day,
Young faces all aglow;
Santa's on his way
O'er the ice and snow.
Jolly Santa Claus,
His whiskers snowy white.
He's happy, boys and girls, because
He'll see you all tonight.

– Arthur Kaser, 1940

Jolly old Saint Nicholas,
Lean your ear this way!
Don't you tell a single soul
What I'm going to say;

Christmas Eve is coming soon;
Now, you dear old man,
Whisper what you'll bring to me;
Tell me if you can.

– *Santa Claus Christmas Book*, 1926

Printed in Germany, 1907

Merrily, merrily, merrily oh!

The reindeer prance across the snow;

We hear their tinkling silver bells,

Whose merry music softly tells

Old Santa Claus is coming.

– *Folk Tales from Many Lands*, 1926

Printed in Germany, 1926

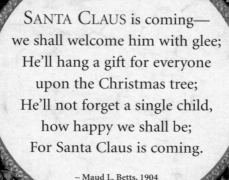

SANTA CLAUS is coming—
we shall welcome him with glee;
He'll hang a gift for everyone
upon the Christmas tree;
He'll not forget a single child,
how happy we shall be;
For Santa Claus is coming.

– Maud L. Betts, 1904

A Joyful Christmas

He's coming with his gifts
For all good girls and boys,
You'll hear his sleigh on Christmas Eve,
Oh, don't you make a noise.
Just hang your stockings up,
And softly go to rest,
On Christmas morning you will find
Just what you like the best.

– Mabel L. Brown, 1904

Silk postcard printed in Germany, 1902

We have trimmed the tree with tinsel;
it is shining in the light,
We have hung our stockings neatly
near the fireplace warm and bright,
We will give a rousing welcome
when he visits us tonight,
We love old Santa Claus.

– Effie Crawford

*M*errily, merrily, now we go!
We've hung our stockings in a row;
Into our beds we'll softly creep,
Just shut our eyes and go to sleep
And wait for Santa Claus' coming.

– Unknown

Illustrated by A. L. Bowley, 1910

Christmas Eve,

four stockings hanging
In a row along the wall,
How reluctantly we left them,
Yet so sure of Santa's call.

Oh, to have that trusting spirit—
Perfect faith, a faith that draws
Us to hope, like in the Yule Time,
When we looked for Santa Claus.

– *Christmas Book for Rural Schools,* 1940

Printed in Germany

I do hope dear, old Santa
Will come this way tonight,
And come here to my stocking,
To fill it nice and tight.

I'd like to watch and see him,
But I know I must wait
Till shines the Christmas sunshine—
I hope he won't be late.

– Alice Kellog, 1902

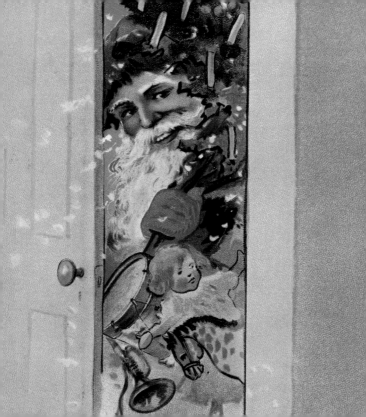

LITTLE CANDLE SPREAD YOUR RAY,

MAKE HIS PATHWAY LIGHT AS DAY;

LET EACH DOOR BE OPENED WIDE

FOR THIS GUEST OF CHRISTMASTIDE.

– Christmas postcard, 1912

Christmas time is here,
Oh, how happy we should be;
All should be good cheer;
Hearts all filled with glee.
Santa's set to go
With packs and packs of toys.
His reindeer dashing through the snow
To sleepy girls and boys.

– Arthur Kaser, 1940

1896 book cover by McLoughlin Brothers, New York

The Night
BEFORE
CHRISTMAS
OR A VISIT OF ST. NICHOLAS.

©
McLOUGHLIN BROS.
INCORPORATED
NEW YORK

Illustration from
The Night Before Christmas
printed by McLoughlin Brothers, 1896

He comes in the night! He comes in the night!
He softly, silently comes;
While the little brown heads on the pillows so white
Are dreaming of bugles and drums.
He cuts through the snow like a ship through the foam,
While the white flakes around him whirl;
Who tells him I know not, but he findeth the home
Of each good little boy and girl.

— John H. Yates, 1912

There's never a home so low, no doubt,

But I in my flight can find it out;

Nor a hut so hidden but I can see

The shadow cast by the lone elm tree!

There's never a home so proud and high

That I am constrained to pass it by;

Nor a heart so happy it may not be

Happier still when blessed by me!

– *The New Christmas Book*, 1912

Illustrated by
A. L. Bowley, 1910

Santa's coat is stuffed full of candy,
While all sorts of beautiful toys
You'll see sticking out of his pockets,
For girls just as well as for boys.

And presents he brings for the mothers
And fathers and aunts with the rest;
But most he will bring for the children,
Because he likes little folks best.

– *Santa Claus Visit*, 1890

77

Raise a festive Christmas tree
With the stars for candles;
Santa's arrival is met with glee,
Please bless each gift he handles.

– Edmund Vance Cooke, 1920

German postcards, 1910

It is good to
be children
sometimes, and
never better
than at
Christmas.

– Charles Dickens

A Merry Christmas

Illustrated by
A. L. Bowley for
Raphael Tuck & Sons
Art Publishers, 1910

DESIGN COPYRIGHTED BY RAPHAEL

Down through the chimney with lots of toys, All for the little ones, Christmas Joys!

– "Up On the House-top,"
Santa Claus Christmas Book,
1926

Best Christmas Wishes

His eyes—how they twinkled!

His dimples, how merry!

His cheeks were like roses,

His nose like a cherry.

– Clement C. Moore, 1822

84

Printed in Germany, 1913

$\mathcal{O}$h, merry, merry,
now are we,

Here's Santa Claus to meet us;

Our Christmas joys are
now complete

Since he has come to greet us.

– *Choice Christmas Entertainments,* 1924

Printed in Germany, 1906

The little red stockings he silently fills,

Till the stockings will hold no more;

The bright little sleds for the great snow hills

Are quickly set down on the floor.

Then Santa Claus mounts to the roof like a bird,

And glides to his seat in the sleigh;

Not the sound of a bugle or drum is heard

As he noiselessly gallops away.

– *The New Christmas Book,* 1912

A Merry Christmas

My busy day

Printed in the United States, 1915

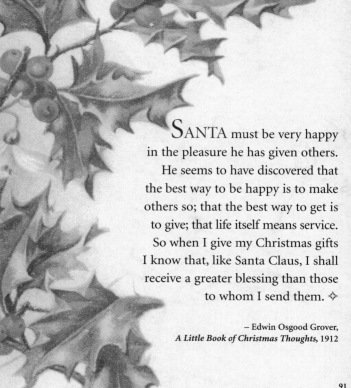

SANTA must be very happy
in the pleasure he has given others.
He seems to have discovered that
the best way to be happy is to make
others so; that the best way to get is
to give; that life itself means service.
So when I give my Christmas gifts
I know that, like Santa Claus, I shall
receive a greater blessing than those
to whom I send them. ✧

– Edwin Osgood Grover,
A Little Book of Christmas Thoughts, 1912

At Christmas we must
remember to do our part;
It is the time of times,
to give with all our heart.

We must always share our joys
with those who have no part,
When Santa Claus is coming.

– Maud L. Betts, 1904

*A*s time shall onward go,

May we, dear Santa grow

Like you each year!

With Christmas love aglow,

May we your spirit show,

Till everyone shall know

The Christmas cheer.

– *The Primary Christmas Book,* 1922

Printed in Germany

And I heard him exclaim
As he drove out of sight,
Merry Christmas to all,
And to all a good night!

– Clement C. Moore, 1822